# Holi

Festivals Around the World

Words in **bold** can be found in the glossary on page 24.

©2016
Book Life
King's Lynn
Norfolk PE30 4LS

ISBN: 978-1-910512-59-3

Written by:
Grace Jones
Edited by:
Amy Allatson
Designed by:
Matt Rumbelow

A catalogue record for this book
is available from the British Library.

# Holi

## Festivals Around the World

Hello, my name is Prita.

When you see Prita, she will tell you how to say a word.

# What is a Festival?

A festival takes place when people come together to celebrate a special event or time of the year. Some festivals last for only one day and others

Some people celebrate festivals by having a party with their family and friends. Others celebrate by holding special events, performing dances or playing music.

# What is Hinduism?

Hinduism is a **religion** that began in India over four thousand years ago. Hindus believe in one god called Brahman. Although, Hindus pray to many different gods and godesses who they believe are forms of Brahman.

**Prita says:**
BRA-MUN (Brahman)

GANESH, ONE OF THE HINDU GODS.

6

Hindus pray to their different gods and goddesses in a temple, called a mandir. Before they enter a mandir, each person must wash so they are clean and remove their shoes as a sign of respect to God.

# What is Holi?

Holi is a festival that is celebrated by Hindus in the spring of every year.

A HINDU TEMPLE IN MADURAI, INDIA.

Holi celebrations usually last for two days.

Holi is also called the 'Festival of Colours'.

Hindus come together to celebrate the start of spring. They celebrate by lighting large bonfires and covering their friends and family in brightly coloured powder and water.

# The Story of Holi

A long, long time ago in India, there was once a great king called Hiranyakashyap. He wanted his people to worship him like a god.

His son, Prahlad, refused and continued to worship the Hindu god, Vishnu. The cruel king punished his son, but still he refused to worship the king.

To learn how to say these words, look on page 24.

The king's sister, a witch named Holika, decided to help the king. She tricked Prahlad into sitting on a burning fire. Holika told him that her magic would protect him.

As the flames grew higher, Vishnu took Prahlad from the fire and saved him from harm. His wicked aunt, Holika, died.

Prahlad felt sorry for his aunt and promised to name a festival after her. The festival Holi, is named after Prahlad's aunt, Holika.

# Lighting Bonfires

At the start of Holi, Hindus light bonfires after sunset to remind them of Holika's story. Also, it is to celebrate Prahlad's **faith** in God.

The lighting of bonfires at Holi is known as Holika Dahan.

Shredded coconuts and rice are thrown on to the bonfires as gifts to God. People gather around the fire and sing and dance together to celebrate the start of Holi.

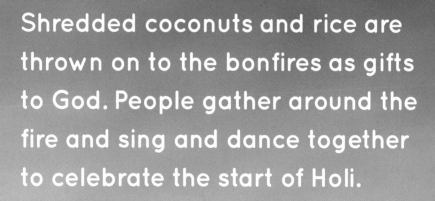

**Prita Says:**
**HO-LEE-KA DA-HAN**
**(Holika Dahan)**

# Festival of Colours

The day after the Holika bonfire, people celebrate Holi by throwing coloured powders and water over each other. They use their hands, balloons and even water guns to cover people in colour!

COLOURED POWDER PAINT

Hindu people wish each other 'Holi Mubarak' which means 'Happy Holi' in Hindi. (HO-LEE MOO-BAH-RAK)

Holi is a time of festive fun, laughter and enjoyment. People play jokes on each other to celebrate the playful God, Krishna. Legend has it that Krishna once played a trick on a group of milkmaids by covering them in coloured water.

# Music and Dancing

People fill the streets with joyful singing and lively dancing to celebrate Holi together as a community. People perform dances, plays and songs that act out the stories of Holika and Krishna.

Traditional instruments, like the dholak, are played in the streets. A dholak is a traditional hand drum. People also blow whistles and sing during the festival.

Prita says:
DO-LUK (Dholak)

# Festive Food

People clean the colours off themselves and come together with their family and friends to eat traditional festival food. In India, **gujiya** – sweet dumplings filled with dry fruit and coconut – are eaten.

Gujiya

Savoury foods, like dahi bhalle, are also eaten during the festival. Dahi bhalle are fried lentil balls that are eaten with yoghurt and different sorts of chutneys.

Prita says:
GUD-JEE-YA (Gujiya)
DU-HE BULL-EE (Dahi Bhalle)

# Love and Forgiveness

Holi is a festival about having fun, but also forgiveness too. It is a time when people put their differences aside, forget old arguments and love one another.

At this time of year, everyone comes together and celebrates with their community and their loved ones. This is why Holi is also called the 'festival of love'.

# Prita Says...

**Brahman**
**Prita says "BRA-MUN"**
Brahman is the true Hindu God.

**Dahi bhalle**
**Prita says "DU-HE BULL-EE"**
Dahi Bhalle are fried lentil balls.

**Dholak**
**Prita says "DO-LUK"**
A dholak is a traditional hand drum.

**Gujiya**
**Prita says "GUD-JEE-YA"**
Gujiya are sweet dumplings filled with dry fruit and coconut.

**Hiranyakashyap**
**Prita says "HE-RAN-NAKER-SHIP"**
Hiranyakashyap was a great king in India.

**Holi Mubarak**
**Prita says "HO-LEE MOO-BAH-RAK"**
Holi Mubarak means 'Happy Holi' in Hindi.

**Holika Dahan**
**Prita says "HO-LEE-KA DA-HAN"**
Holika Dahan is the tradtion of lighting bonfires during Holi.

**Prahlad**
**Prita says "PRA-LAD"**
Prahlad was the great king, Hiranyakashyap's son.

**Vishnu**
**Prita says "VISH-NOO"**
Vishnu is one of the many Hindu Gods.

# Glossary

**Faith:** belief in a god(s).

**Religion:** a set of beliefs based around a god(s).

**Savoury:** food which is salty or spicy and not sweet.

**Traditional:** something that is passed from person to person over a long time.

**Worship:** a religious act, such as praying.

# Index

# Credits

Photocredits: Abbreviations: l-left, r-right, b-bottom, t-top, c-centre, m-middle. All images are courtesy of Shutterstock.com. Front Cover — AJP. 1 – AJP, 2 – Yavuz Sariyildiz, 4 – Tom Wang, 5 – imagedb.com, 6 – Tatyana Prokofieva, 7 – LiliGraphie, 8 – Noradoa, 9 – Yavuz Sariyildiz, 10l – AJP, 10r – RonTech3000, 12 – Anatoli Styf, 13 – Anna Jurkovska, 14 – Rajesh Narayanan, 15 – AJP, 16 – Pikoso.kz, 17 – imagedb.com, 18 – GreenTree, 19 – Mukesh Kumar, 20 – imagedb.com, 21 – Ailisa,